LITTLE BOOK OF

Sewing

With Fiona Hesford

at The Gilliangladrag Fluff-a-torium

GILLiANGLADRAG

LITTLE BOOK OF

Sewing

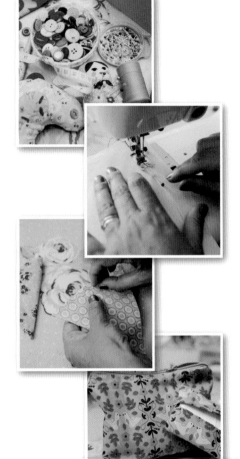

First published in the UK in 2014

© Demand Media Limited 2014

www.demand-media.co.uk

Printed and bound in Europe

ISBN 978-1-910270-82-0

The views in this book are those of the author but they are general views only and readers are urged to consult the relevant and qualified specialist for individual advice in particular situations.

Demand Media Limited hereby exclude all liability to the extent permitted by law of any errors or omissions in this book and for any loss, damage or expense (whether direct or indirect) suffered by a third party relying on any information contained in this book.

All our best endeavours have been made to secure copyright clearance for every photograph used but in the event of any copyright owner being overlooked please address correspondence to Demand Media Limited, Waterside Chambers, Bridge Barn Lane, Woking, Surrey, GU21 6NL.

Contents

Chapter 1

Sewing Tips

Keep children safe and away from the sewing area.

Be safe when using a sewing machine, keep fingers away from needle area when in action.

Its a good idea to have a clean bright area or room dedicated to your sewing, it saves you having to clear away in the middle of a project, with one table for laying out and cutting and a separate one for your machine.

Be organised using see through plastic boxes allows you to see what you have quickly. Have your equipment close to hand when working and why not stick a small paper bag to the table a handy bin for off cuts.

Remember to always pin fabric with the raw edges on the right hand side and the pin head towards you and keep to your required seam allowance ie the distance away from the raw edge. Finish all raw edges to avoid fraying with pinking shears or zig zag stitch.

Trim ends before sewing to avoid them getting caught up in the machine.

If your sewing gets stuck in the machine, remove all fabric, clear all threads and start again, always have the needle in the highest position when removing from the machine.

Make your own pin cushion using scraps of fabric and fill with lentils.

Start your own fabric stash, save money by using old cut up clothes, curtains, fabric swatches and bedlinen and recycle buttons zips and trims.

Up cycle clothing by adding pockets, trims, collars, or appliqué a design, let your creativity run riot.

Keep your machine well maintained by giving it a regular service and treat it to some oil. occasionally i.e. dab some machine oil on to a brush and coat any visible moving part.

Chapter 2

Sewing Equipment

Its a good idea to stock up on some basic equipment before you get started.

Here is a guide to the items recommended when beginning to sew...

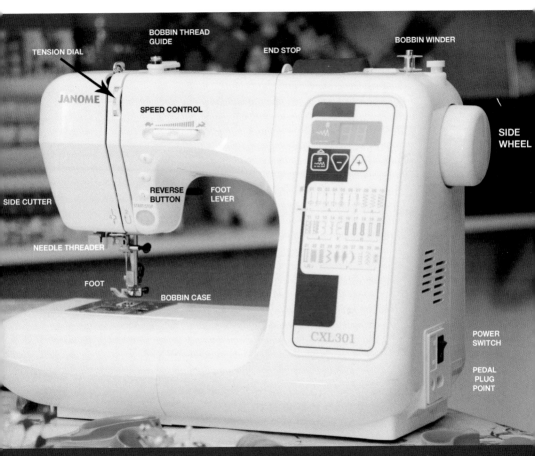

SEWING MACHINE: (top or front loader). Look out for one with a side cutter, an auto needle threader a removable front table and seam allowance markings.

Fabric Types:

When starting to sew, choose inexpensive fabrics to start with and consider the type of fabric needed for the project you are undertaking.

For example if you are doing some bunting or a gathered skirt for example, choose lightweight fabrics such as cotton, polyester cotton, viscose.

For projects such as cushions, patchwork, throws, table runners or more structured clothes such as an A-Line skirt or an unlined dress, you need medium weight fabrics.

When sewing bags or storage containers or garden cushions, heavier weight fabrics are best for durability, choose denim, canvas, cotton duck, corduroy or upholstery fabric.

Some fabrics have a pile, ie they have a soft carpet like feel such as velvet, corduroy. These fabrics are best steamed rather than pressed with an iron and have a direction to them (nap) so take care when matching up pieces.

Fabrics such as felt and fleece don't fray at the edges when cut, so are good fabrics for starter projects.

Satin fabric is shiny and frays quite easily, but is cheap and effective especially when sewing costumes.

Stretch fabric such as jersey or lycra is good for close fitting projects.

Other tools :

Stitch Ripper or Stitch Unpick: this is invaluable for undoing seams quickly by slicing through stitches.

Tape Measure and ruler and a fabric marker or a soft pencil

Hand sewing needles: have a selection of different sizes with small and large eyes for easy threading.

Machine needles: have a selection of assorted sizes and use the appropriate needle for your fabric type.

Needle Threader: (for hand sewing needles only) pass the wire loop through the eye of the needle and drop the thread in to the loop and pull through. They are quite fragile so handle with care.

Thimble: this is a finger protector when hand sewing.

Pinking Shears: good quality shears will last a lifetime so keep sharp by folding tinfoil in half then quarter and cut into several times.

Pins: choose sharp ones with a bead head and a pin cushion is also useful.

Velcro: for using with fabric use sew on velcro.

Buttons: a pack of assorted colours and sizes is easily available.

Threads: A range of inexpensive 1000m reels of threads in an assortment of colours will mean you always have a suitable thread and plenty of it! Other specialist threads available include extra strong thread, quilting thread, topstitch thread, invisible thread, machine embroidery thread, these can all be used on a machine.

Trims: ribbons of all kinds are inspiring as well as ric rac trims, fringes, lace, beading and pom pom trims to name but a few. Its a good idea to get a mixed assorted bag to get you started.

Bias Binding or seam binding: this is a folded strip of fabric sold by the metre which has been cut on the cross grain of the fabric to allow stretch. Useful for bunting or finishing raw edges and hems.

Zips: dress zips, concealed zips, open ended zips and continuous zipping (for cushions).

Wadding: this is used when making a quilt and is sold by the metre in a selection of thicknesses and available in polyester or natural fibres.

Toy Stuffing/ cushion pads: have some to hand or a pad or two for when making cushions.

Interfacing: Useful for adding thickness to fabrics, available in fusible or non-fusible types. Iron on fusible interfacing to the reverse side of fabrics.

Bonding web: suitable for use when doing an applique shape.

A Poker: useful for poking out corners use a chunky knitting needle or a chopstick and keep close to hand.

Magnetic Seam Guide: this clamps on to the metal plate of the machine and helps you to sew straight and keep to your seam allowance.

Masking tape: is good for marking fabrics and holding ribbons and trims secure when stitching them in place.

Scissors: Buy the best quality you can afford with moulded or soft handles. A small pair of embroidery scissors and a pair of thread cutters is useful too.

Chapter 3.

How the Machine Works

Wind the bobbin...

Place thread on the spool rod and secure with an end stop if needed.
Place bobbin on to the bobbin winder at top.

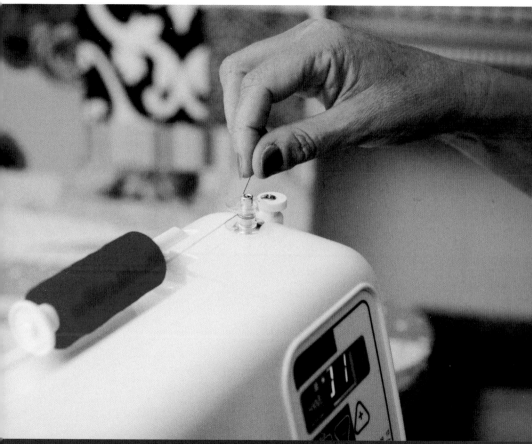

Pass thread end under the disc at top and wind it round a bobbin a few times.
Push across into action and press pedal to wind bobbin up.

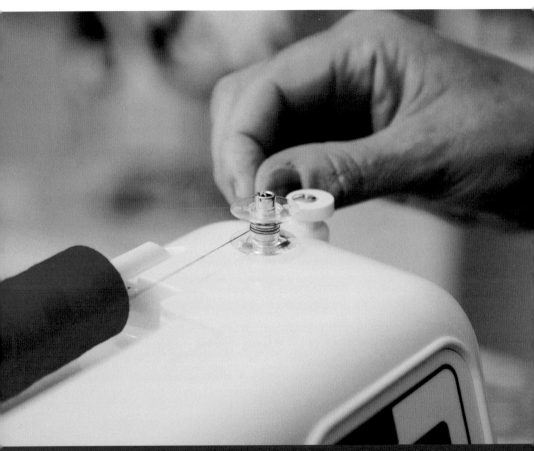

When complete, push the bobbin across, lift off and cut the thread. Drop the bobbin into the bobbin case and slide the thread under the metal flap. For front loading machines refer to manual.

Thread the needle...

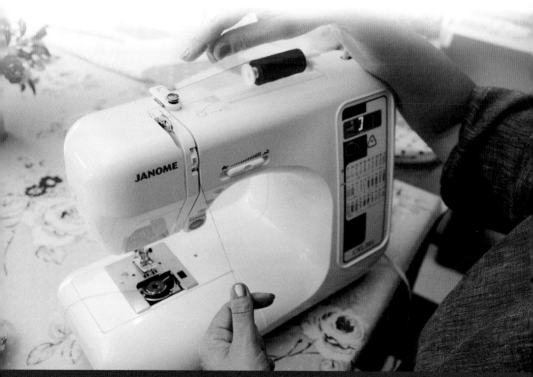

Slide the thread around and down the first section 1 then up section 2, over the metal hook
at section 3 (wind the side dial to lift needle up exposing the hook) then down to section 4.

Pass behind small hook at top of needle then pass thread through the eye of the needle from front to back

Holding the needle thread with your left hand, draw the bobbin thread up using the side dial (wind towards you so needle drops down and up once) a loop will appear so pull through then extend out beyond the machine about 10cms. Pass both threads under the foot and out to the back. Replace the bobbin cover.

Stitch Settings...

Make sure tension dial is set to 4 and stitch setting is programmed to straight stitch with length set between 2 to 3.

Chapter 4

Practice Stitches

Sewing a straight line,
a curve, a corner
and reverse stitching...

Place fabric on the machine and lower foot (using the foot lever). Sew a straight line, then a curve by gently turning fabric from one side to the other. Sew a corner by lifting foot of the machine with the needle down, turn, then lower foot and continue. Practise sewing forwards and backwards just a few stitches at a time. Lift foot of machine with needle at highest point to remove fabric, cut thread. Leave approx 10cm of thread extended beyond the machine.

Chapter 5

Seams & Edges

Sewing a Seam...

Pin fabric together at sides so that raw edges are matched up and pin head towards you with raw edge on the RHS. Place on machine with raw edge at RHS and lower the needle at the top of the fabric at the required seam allowance. Lower the foot, stitch forwards and backwards a few stitches, continue straight to the end of the fabric then stitch backwards and forwards a few stitches thus reinforcing the end stitches.

Finishing the Raw Edges...

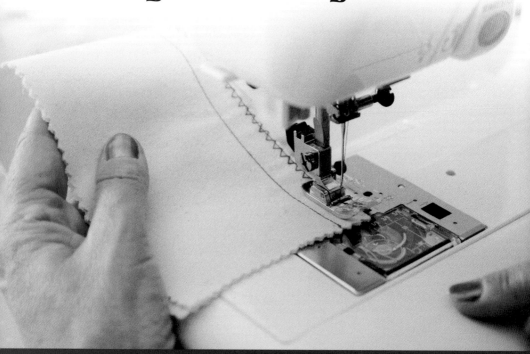

Cut the raw edge using pinking shears or sew a line of zig zag stitches along the raw edge. To do this, set the machine to zig zag stitch at maximum width, then place the raw edge at the centre of the foot, stitch along so that the zig zag stitch binds the raw edge all along the length of the seam. Remove from machine. Tie ends together each side and trim.

Chapter 6

Patchwork Envelope Cushion

1. Cut out your cotton fabric squares using a paper template **(for a 30cm cushion use 9 squares of 12cm x 12cm)**. Arrange in 3 rows and 3 columns in the order you would like them to be. Fold over and pin together the outer squares with the centre square with the right sides of fabric facing. Stitch with a 1cm seam allowance so you have 3 strips of 3 squares.

2. Iron seams flat, then lay on a table. Pin together long sides of each patchwork strip with right sides of fabric facing together and seams matching.

3. Stitch with a 1cm seam allowance.

4. Press seams open.

Envelope style backing...

(For a 30cm cushion you need 2 pieces of fabric 32cm x 25cm in size for the backing).

5. Fold over and press 1cm then fold again and press 2cm on one long side of both back pieces. Stitch along the edge of the inner fold to make a hem.

6. Place front piece on a table with right side facing up, place one back piece face down on top with hem at centre, raw edges matching. Repeat for other side. Pin then stitch all around with a 1cm seam allowance.

7. Finish raw edges, trim across corners, turn cushion to right side, push out corners.

8. Insert cushion pad. Lovely!

9. **Optional buttonhole:** Stitch a buttonhole and button or sew on velcro if desired.

Chapter 7

Bunting (2 ways)

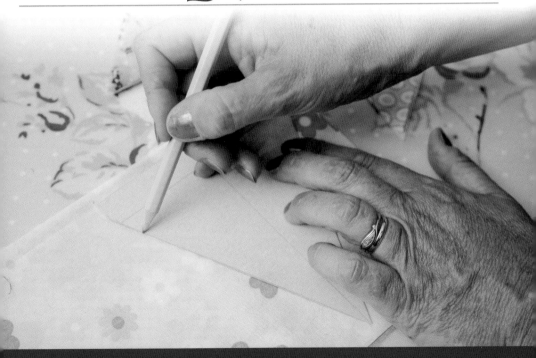

1. Draw around a template made from cardboard on to two pieces of fabric per flag.

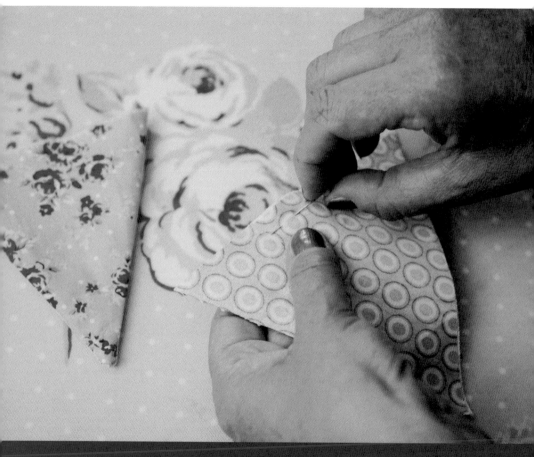

2. Pin the triangles together at slanted sides with the right sides of fabric facing each other.

3. Sew with a 1cm seam down the slanted edges, trim the corner and turn inside out push out corners with a poker.

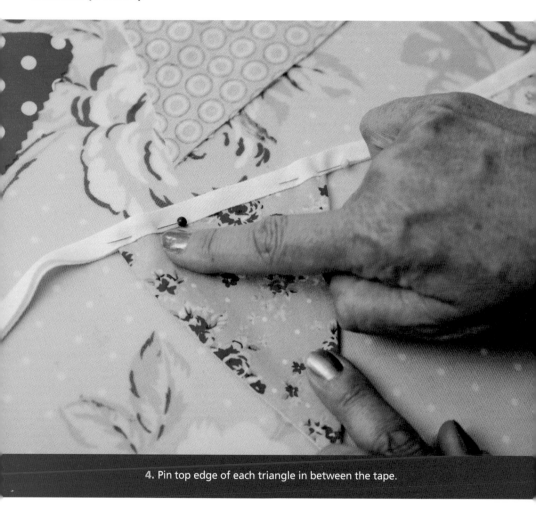

4. Pin top edge of each triangle in between the tape.

5. Stitch along the tape.

6. Attach a button and a loop at each end.
(For simple quick bunting use one triangle piece per flag and attach to tape as described).

Chapter 8.

Lined tote bag

1. Cut out 2 squares for bag outer (front and back) and 2 lining pieces (the same size) and 2 handles from webbing (or you could make fabric ones).

2. Pin the handles into the top edge, equal distance from the centre point.

3. Stitch across close to the top edge (ie 5mm) and remove pins.

4. Lay the lining piece on top of the bag and match up the raw edges. Pin in place and stitch across from one side to the other with a 1cm seam allowance.

5. Press the seam flat and open.

6. Lay one piece on top of the other matching up the bag and the lining pieces with the right sides of fabric together. Make sure that your side seams are lined up. Stitch all the way around with a 1cm seam allowance leaving an opening in the bottom of the lining for turning of approx 10cm.

7. To make a base for the bag, pull bag apart at the corners, flatten down each corner & pin, draw a line across with a ruler and pencil approx 4cm down from the corner points, then stitch across corner following pencil line from one side to the other.

8. Turn the bag inside out through the opening in the lining and push out the corners.

9. Finally, stitch the opening together in the lining. Press.

Chapter 9

Gathered Elasticated Skirt

with optional ric rac trim and pocket

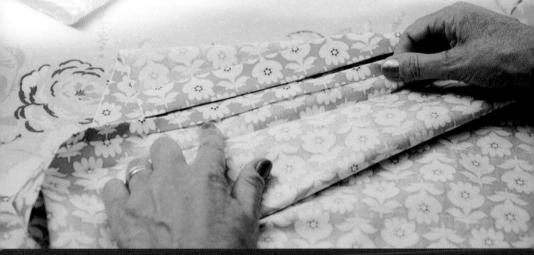

1. Cut a piece of fabric the required skirt length but add on 3cm extra for the hem and 4cm extra for the waistband, the width is 1.5 – 2 times your hip dimensions. Fold over and press 1cm then again 2cm for the bottom hem. Stitch along the hem close to the inner fold.

Ric rac trim (optional)...

2. Stick the ric rac trim down over the line of the stitching with masking tape. Stitch down the centre of the ric rac trim over the tape, then remove.

3. To make a french seam, with the wrong sides of fabric together, pin together at short side. Sew down the side seam with a 1cm seam allowance and trim down to .5cm. Turn inside out with the right sides of the fabric together and pin at side seam. Stitch a 1cm seam along, thus encasing the raw edges.

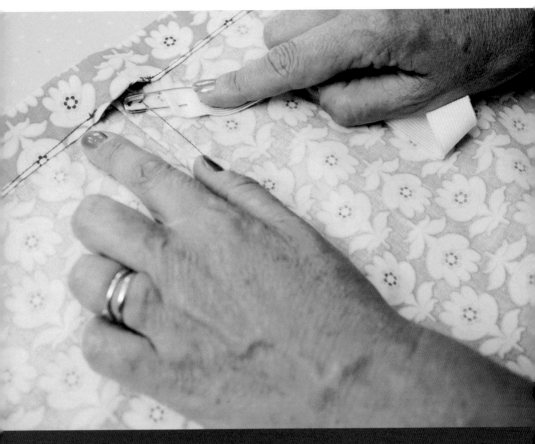

4. At the top edge of skirt, fold over 1cm, press and then fold over 3cms and press and stitch a hem about 5mm away from the inner fold, leaving a 3cm opening at one side seam.

GATHERED ELASTICATED SKIRT

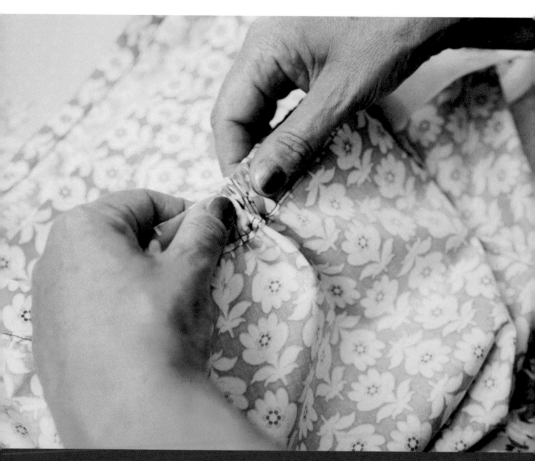

5. Insert the elastic through the opening using a safety pin on the end, and feed through hem all around.

6. Pin elastic together at ends, try on and adjust to fit.

7. Stitch the ends of the elastic together and then stitch the opening up.

Pocket (optional)...

1. Cut a square piece of fabric for pocket 1cm larger all around than required pocket size. Iron on light weight interfacing to the reverse side if you have some. Stitch some seam binding or bias binding to top edge or sew a small hem. Fold over and iron 1cm on the other 3 sides.

GATHERED ELASTICATED SKIRT

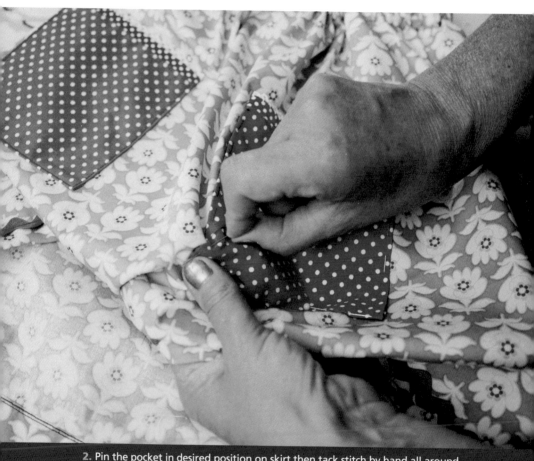

2. Pin the pocket in desired position on skirt then tack stitch by hand all around (tacking is a line of approx 1cm running stitches by hand).

3. On the machine, stitch down the pocket close to the edge on all three sides, reinforcing the top of the pocket with reverse stitches.

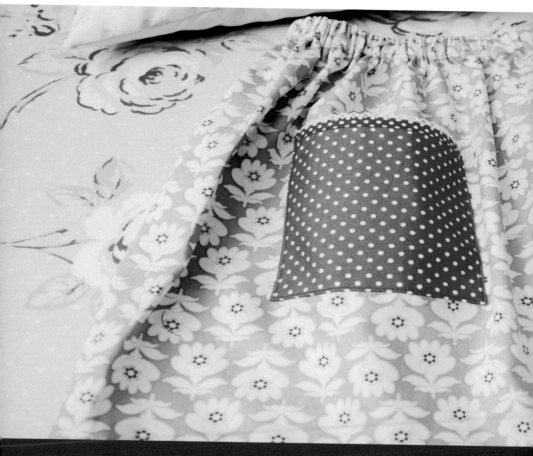

4. Remove the tacking stitches, and sew in the ends. Job done!

Chapter 10

Cosmetic Bag &
Matching Tissue Holder

Cosmetic Bag...

1. Cut 2 pieces of fabric for outer bag and 2 pieces for lining, (this one measures 24cm x 24cm approx).

2. Reinforce your outer fabric with iron on interfacing and then lay one lining piece on the table. Lay one fabric piece on top with wrong sides together.

3. Lay the zip face down on top, with the zip pull facing down and out of the way of the fabric. Tack in place. Stitch from one side to another on the machine with needle position shifted over so it is closer to the zipped teeth, or use a zip foot.

4. Repeat for the other side.

5. Zig zag finish the raw top edges. Pull the zip pull in to the centre of the bag.

6. Pin together the 3 raw edges and stitch down with a 1cm seam from the zip all the way down, across and up. Take care when sewing across the zip and sew some reverse stitches at each far end to reinforce them. Trim and zig zag finish the raw edges.

7. Stitch across the corners at each side, about 2.5cm down from the top point.

8. Turn to right side and push corners out. And there you have it!

Tissue holder...

1. Cut out 2 pieces of outer fabric 9cm x 15cm and two pieces the same size in lining fabric. Place the two lining pieces together, wrong sides together. Fold over and press in half the two outer fabric pieces so the long sides are matching and wrong sides together. Place the two folded pieces on top of lining pieces with fold at centre and raw edges matching up, pin, stitch all around 1cm from edge or line up the side of the foot with the edge of the fabric.

2. Zig zag raw edges then trim corners, turn inside out and push out corners.

3. Insert your tissues and pop inside your cosmetics bag. Gorgeous!

Design & Artwork: ALEX YOUNG

Photography: ED SCHOFIELD

Published by: DEMAND MEDIA LIMITED

Publisher: JASON FENWICK

Written by: FIONA HESFORD